Soto's Song

Soto's Song

Dave Kroner

Photographic Art by Ramona du Houx

Polar Bear & Company
An imprint of the
Solon Center for Research and Publishing
Solon & Rockland, Maine

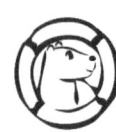

Polar Bear & Company™
Solon Center for Research and Publishing
20 Main Street, Rockland, ME 04841
polarbearandco.org, soloncenter.org
galleryfukurou.com, 207.319.4727

The Solon Center is a 501(c)3 Maine Public Benefit Corporation with the mission of helping to build community and protect the environment through educational and literary means, including the arts, music, and science. Gallery Fukurou is at 20 Main St., Rockland.

Text Copyright © 2021 by David Kroner
Cover design by Ramona du Houx; photo of Dave Kroner by
Lex Bowman. Photo of Ramona du Houx by Paul Cornell du Houx.

All rights reserved. No part of this book may be reproduced in any form without permission in writing from the author, artist, or publisher, except for brief quotations for critical articles and reviews.

ISBN: 978-1-882190-33-1
Premium edition, May 1, 2022
Library of Congress Control Number: 2021935262
Manufactured in the USA on durable, acid-free paper.

Dedicated to all who have found peace, wisdom, and enlightenment on their own personal journeys through apotheosis.

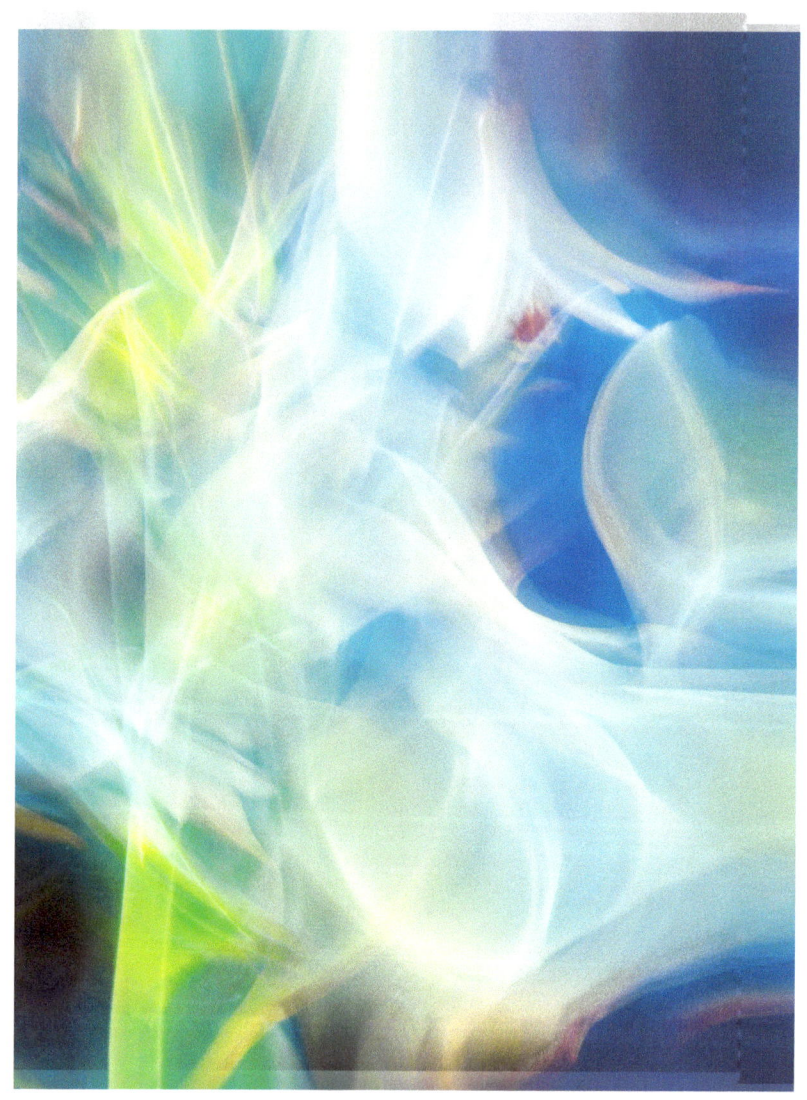

Earthbound Angels

Photographic Art

Earthbound Angels, vi
Stream Harp, viii
Ignite, 3
Spring Embers, 5
Reality, 7
Life, 9
Oak Maine, 11
Nature's Humanity, 13
Life's Trails, 15
Maze DNA, 17
Crystal Cave, 19
Transformation, 21
Lift Off, 23
Spirit Dance, 25
Reach, 27
Spring, 29
Here, 31
Holly, 33
Summer Rush, 35
Lily Dance, 37
Fall, 39
Waterfall Break, 41

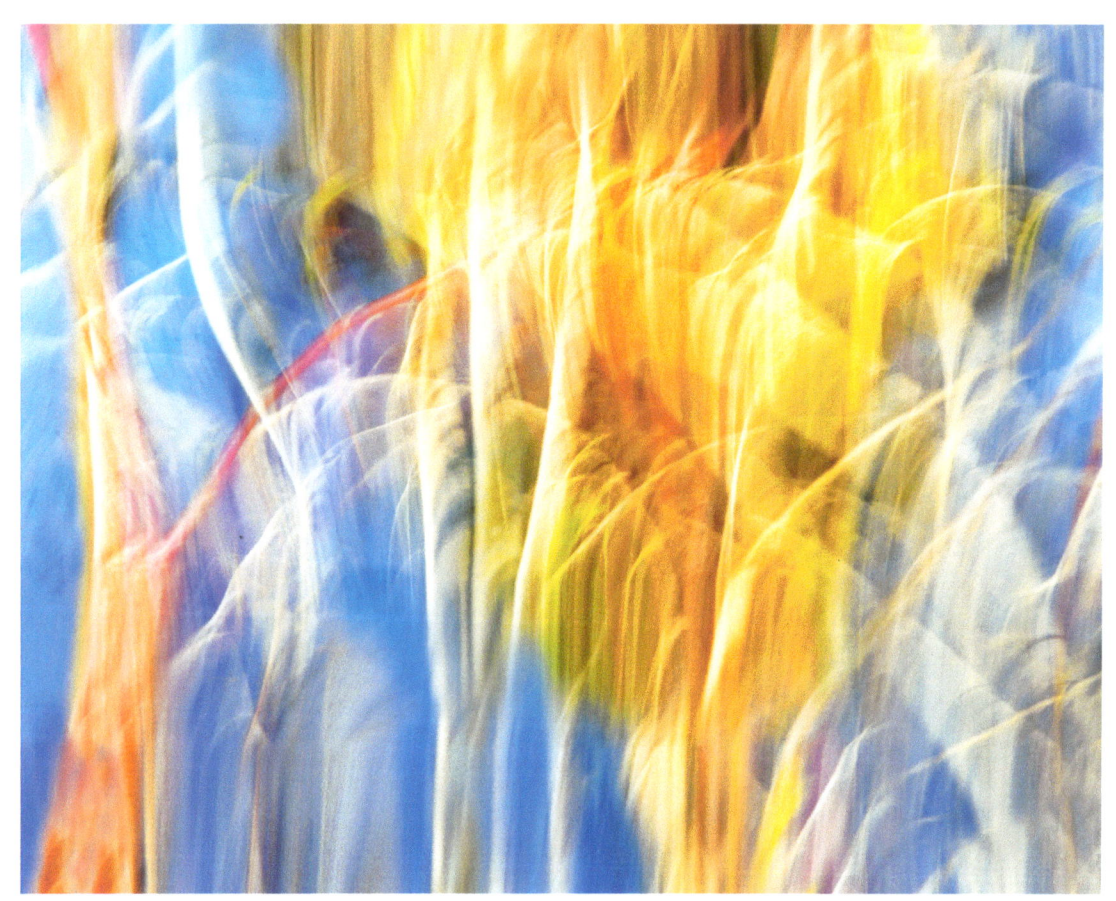

Stream Harp

*M*ANY HAD COME AND MANY HAD GONE, BUT ONLY ONE REMAINED.

In a long-forgotten forest lived Soto, who knew only what Nature had taught him. From the Earth he had come, from the Earth had received his name, and to the stars he was destined.

He lived from what Nature had to offer and spent his days wandering through the forest, whistling tunes the various birds had lent. He collected the sights, sounds, and scents of the natural wonders, as well as items that travelers had lost along their journeys to and from the neighboring village.

Over time, he had acquired quite a collection of unique utensils and other objects that he kept in a large burlap sack smattered with faded patches, which gave an added vitality to his otherwise earthen appearance.

When not wandering through his forest home, finding treasures, Soto found comfort in a small clearing, where brilliant rays played over the deep hues of blue-green mosses and tall grass.

Opening his eyes from a midmorning nap, he stretched the sleep from his body as the warm, caressing glow touched his face, and a gentle spring breeze whispered sweet secrets of the natural world.

Over his weather-worn boots, a careless caterpillar crawled, as if the moving mountains were nothing but an effortless experience in its journey through transformation. Smiling, Soto lent his finger, lifting his unsuspecting friend to the heights of an offering branch.

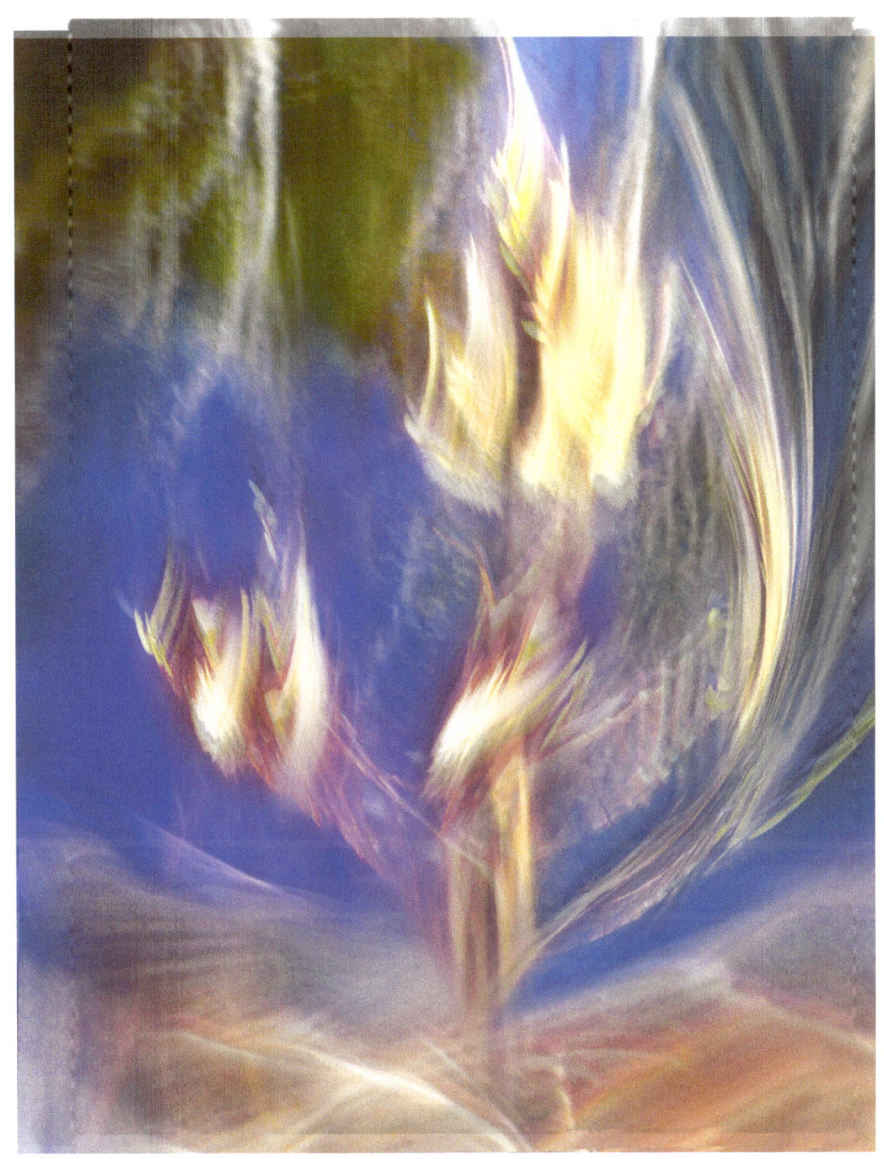

𝒯urning towards the rising east, he tightened with a strange new feeling of adventure that had been aroused from deep within the reality of his dreams—the vigilant flame within had ignited the torch. Soto loved his forest home and animal friends, but was drawn to this new excitement of wonder that caused his heart to sing.

Gathering his thoughts and burlap sack, he whistled the song of a blackbird and proceeded in the direction of the village, to return the treasures, back to the people from whom they had come.

Walking now through great shadows of oaks, Soto came to a rippling brook. Gingerly, he stepped onto a stone at rest and peered down at his diamond-studded reflection; there, just under the surface of the purest tide, reclined a curiosity.

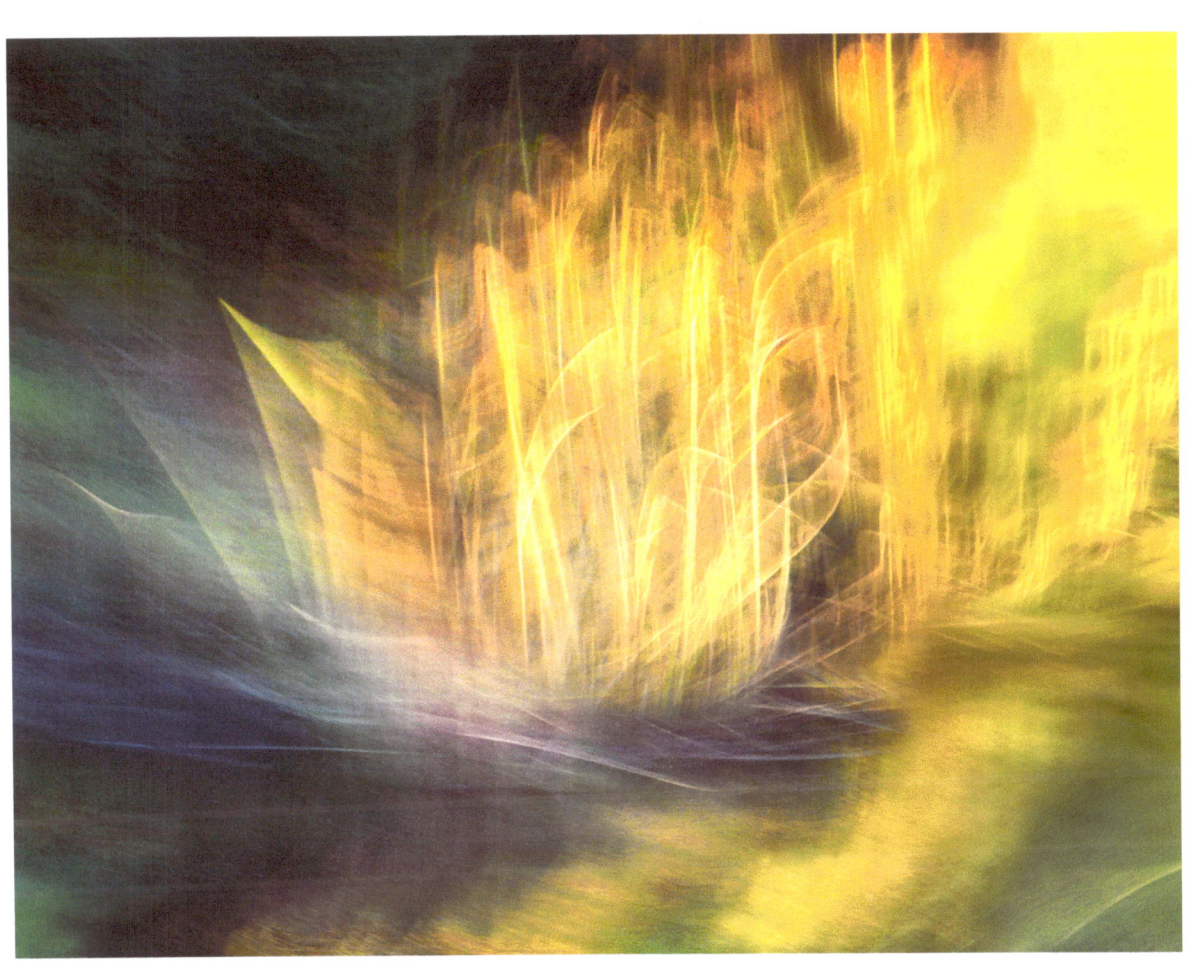

Spring Embers

Reaching down though the surface and scatterings of minnows and tadpoles, he pulled the object into the rich forest air. The delicate features of a flute lay in his palm: a long, wooden cylinder with a mouthpiece of gold. Carved in its smooth body were feathered details. It was the most beautiful instrument Soto had ever discovered. The sparkle in his eyes reflected its golden fiery surfaces.

As the wonder of discovery coursed through his heart, a shadow caused him to peer upwards to glimpse a peacock flutter from the abounding treetops.

The magic and wonders of the forest never ceased to amaze him.

Placing the instrument in his pocket, he carried on.

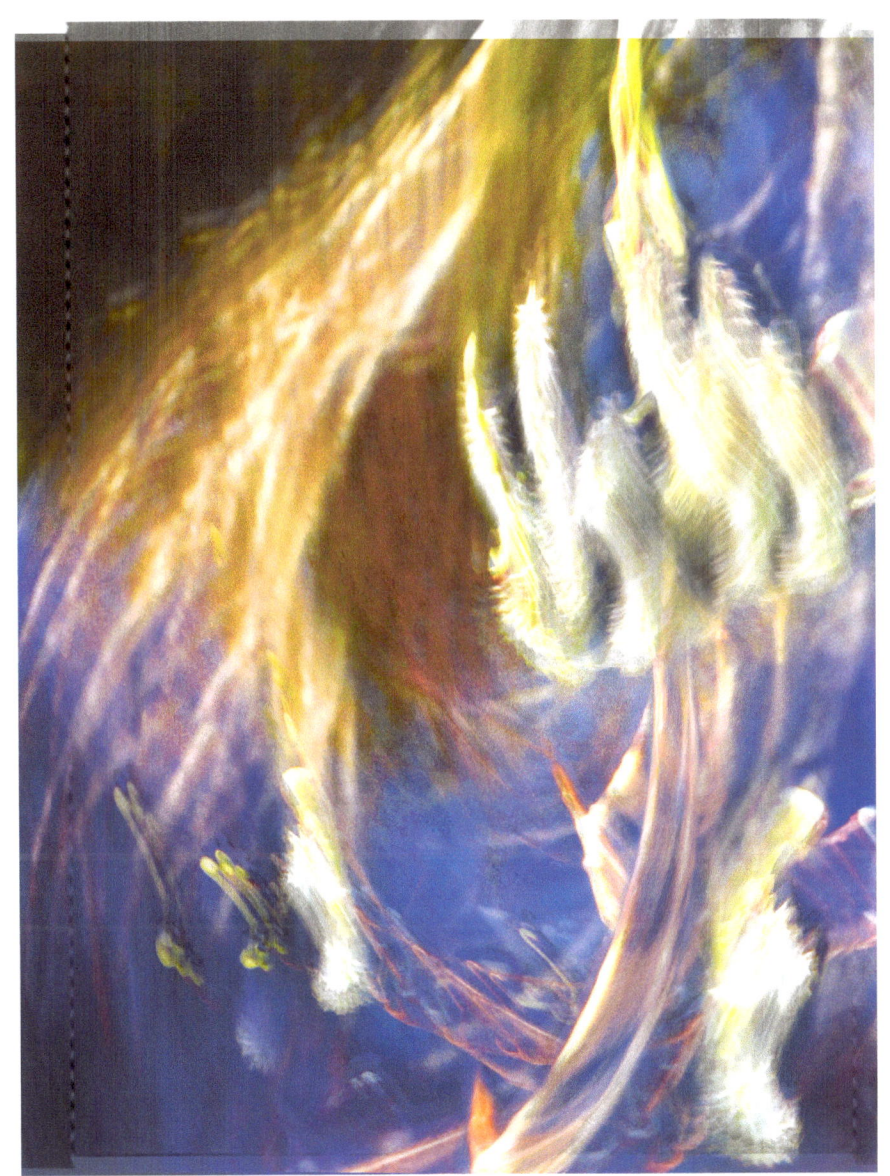

Reality
Reality

*B*reaking the edge of the forest, excitement and curiosity were his companions, but Soto paused to admire the vastness and beauty of the country that stretched to infinity before him.

A willing raven guided him to a well-worn path made by others on a similar journey. He felt an anticipation of experience on the warm breeze that pushed him onward.

Visions of greatness filled Soto's mind, as he traversed rolling hills and lush meadow-scapes, inhaling the scents of dew-covered wildflowers and sun-sweetened fruit trees, carried on the winds that swept through the valleys.

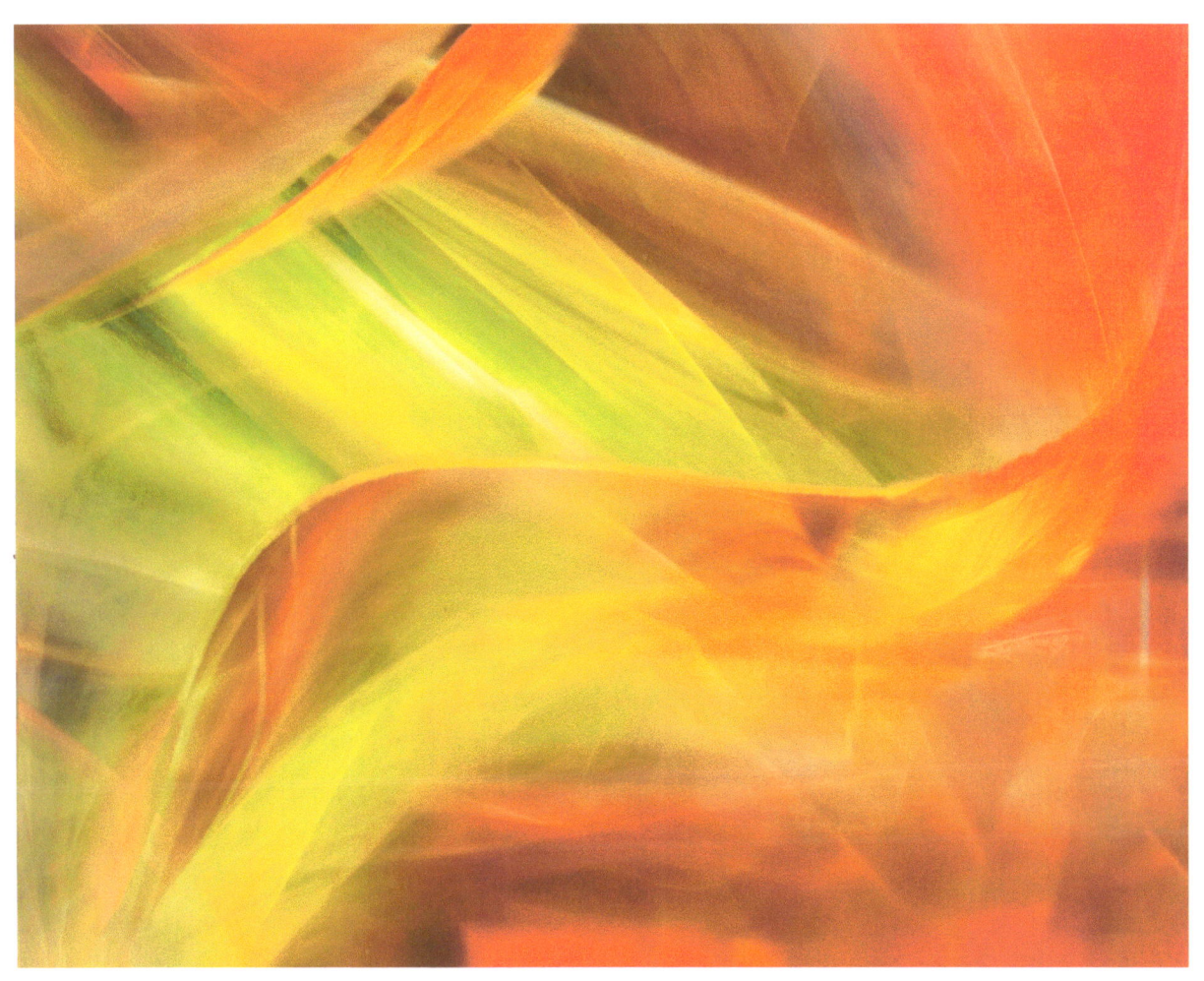

Life

*P*resently lost in his thoughts, Soto had not yet noticed the clear presence of a shadow that had joined him on his journey. He hesitated to breathe, as it swallowed him completely. Slower were Soto's steps as his heartbeat quickened to vibrating. The features of a bear came into sharp focus, and the shadow loomed ever larger.

Feeling its steamy breath on the back of his neck, Soto watched a giant shadow-paw stretch into the air from behind him. As the paw swept downward, he darted outward and upwards to the heights of a neighboring tree.

The frustrated bear, who lacked the sensations of fullness, lumbered over to the base of the tree and pawed fiercely at its trunk, wanting nothing more than to satisfy her ferocious appetite.

Many moments passed for Soto; he had found freedom indulging in the generous fruit the tree provided. Time had faded in and out of consciousness, when thoughts of the flute filled his mind with curiosity. Taking it from his pocket, he placed it to his lips and exhaled into the golden tip. A melody poured forth, and Soto visualized white, wispy strands of magical-music notes swirl down the thick trunk of the tree and around a bemused bear. As the notes danced around the mighty beast, calmness settled in her heart, and heaviness overcame her eyes. Slowly the bear succumbed to a silent slumber.

Taking this opportunity, Soto scurried from his tree and down the path.

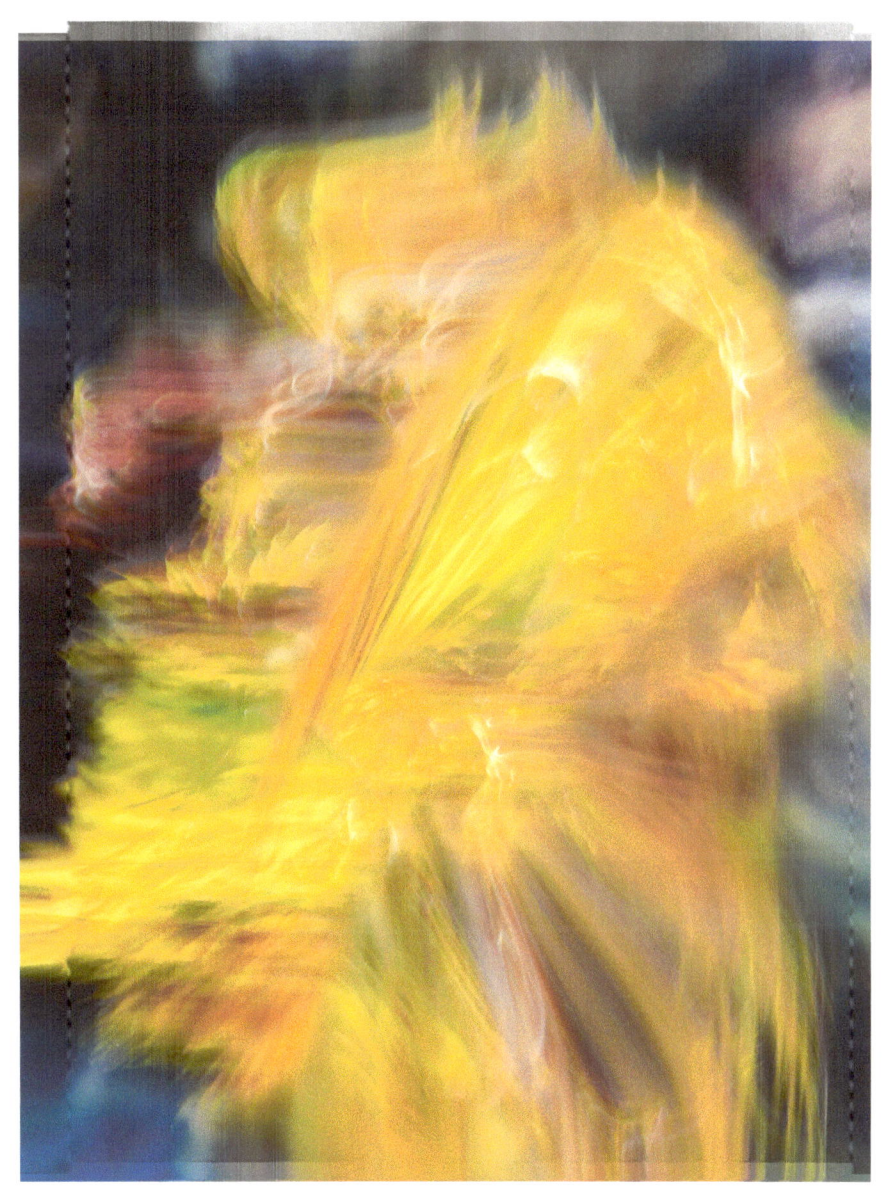

As the early afternoon sun reached its zenith in the vibrant blue sky, and the shadows vanished, Soto felt his body needing a rest. Hearing sweet songs of red birds calling him over to the shade of a willow tree in the distance, he found a soft spot amongst a cluster of fragrant rose bushes. He lay back, propping his head on the patched sack, and stared up, greeting his feathered friends with a cheerful tune.

As he nestled into Nature's caress, Soto heard sounds of unnatural shouting, fast approaching. One glance into the distance spotted a motley group of ruffians, who knew no feelings of kindness, headed in his direction.

Ever closer they came, with fiery, threatening gesture towards Soto and his sack of treasures.

Quickly, he slung the sack over his shoulder and headed in the opposite direction. Making his way through bushes and brambles, he soon found himself caught within lofty cliff walls.

Soto's mind spun with exhilaration at the sounds of this danger that echoed through the valley, as thoughts of the flute sang through his wild mind, and he pulled it from his pocket and placed it to his lips.

The melodious tune filled the valley; the mystical music swirled upwards, caressing vines that clung for life on the rocky walls. A gentle breeze stirred, loosening them enough for Soto to grab hold and climb swiftly up out of harm's way.

Staring down, he saw the ruffians shake their sun-scarred fists at him, as they failed to climb the vines that gave way under earthen-soaked weight.

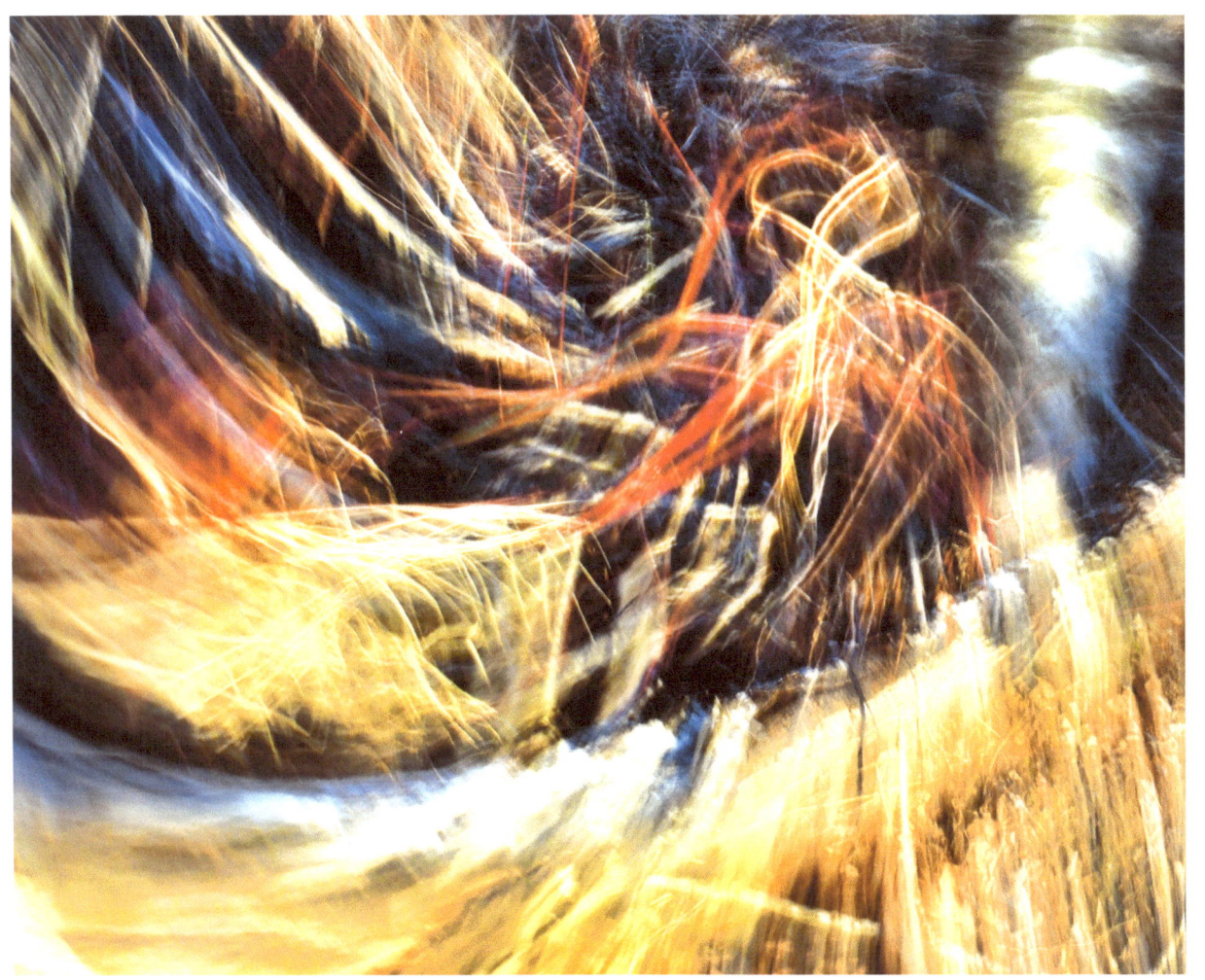

Nature's Humanity

Soto turned to look back over the windswept treetops covering the valley floor in a quilt of the most delicate fabrics in Nature and was captivated by the beauty of all he beheld.

The day proceeded, his journey progressed, shifting scenery in the late afternoon glow of a glorious sun. Colors deepened to those of hope, scents strengthened to those of determination, and sweet sounds emerged to those of anticipation in the heart of Mother Nature.

Beckoning rooftops of the village peeked over rolling hills in the distance, bringing a spring back to his step, knowing his destination was near.

Finding himself on an untrammeled path, Soto carried on, as the song in his heart poured out through the tune on his lips.

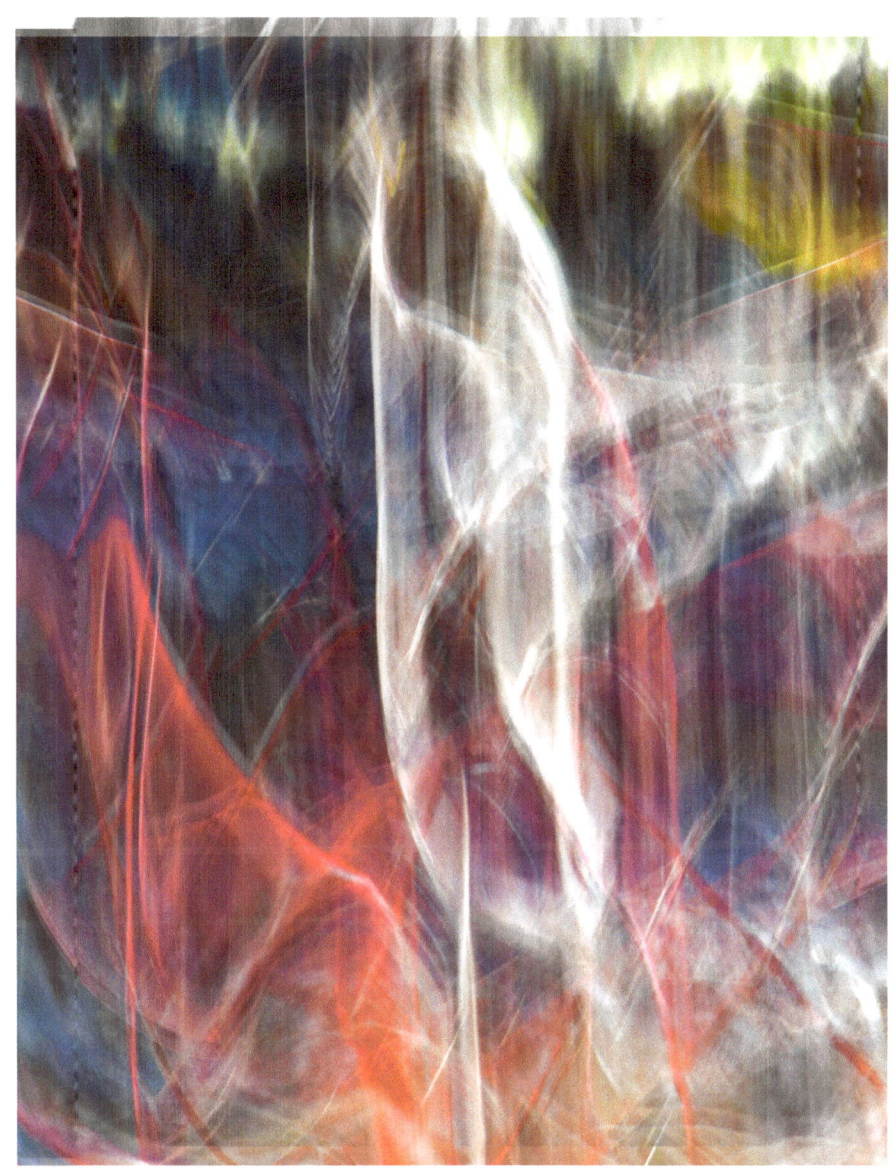

Life's Trails

*F*eeling strength from within radiate into the space around him, Soto was aware of how Nature reflected his thoughts and responded now with a current racing through river waters before him.

He watched in wonder at the speed and life that teamed in this indigo world below.

Knowing he would be swept away by its restless waters, who knew not his limited boundaries, Soto brought out the flute and let his heart play a tune. As time passed, the waters receded enough to reveal river-smooth stones, providing a natural bridge for him to cross.

With the weightlessness of wonder in his thoughts, he strolled along through the terrain until, yet again, he found himself within the long grasp of Nature's grip. He had come to the edge of a forest so full of natural wonders that it left room for little else, save the shadows that hid its beauty. The tight tree trunks left only enough space for sight to penetrate a ways into the deep blackness holding fast to treasures that knew no warmth or strength of the setting sun.

Soto stepped back and swept his eyes from side to side and saw the magnitude, the multitude of options that stood before his question.

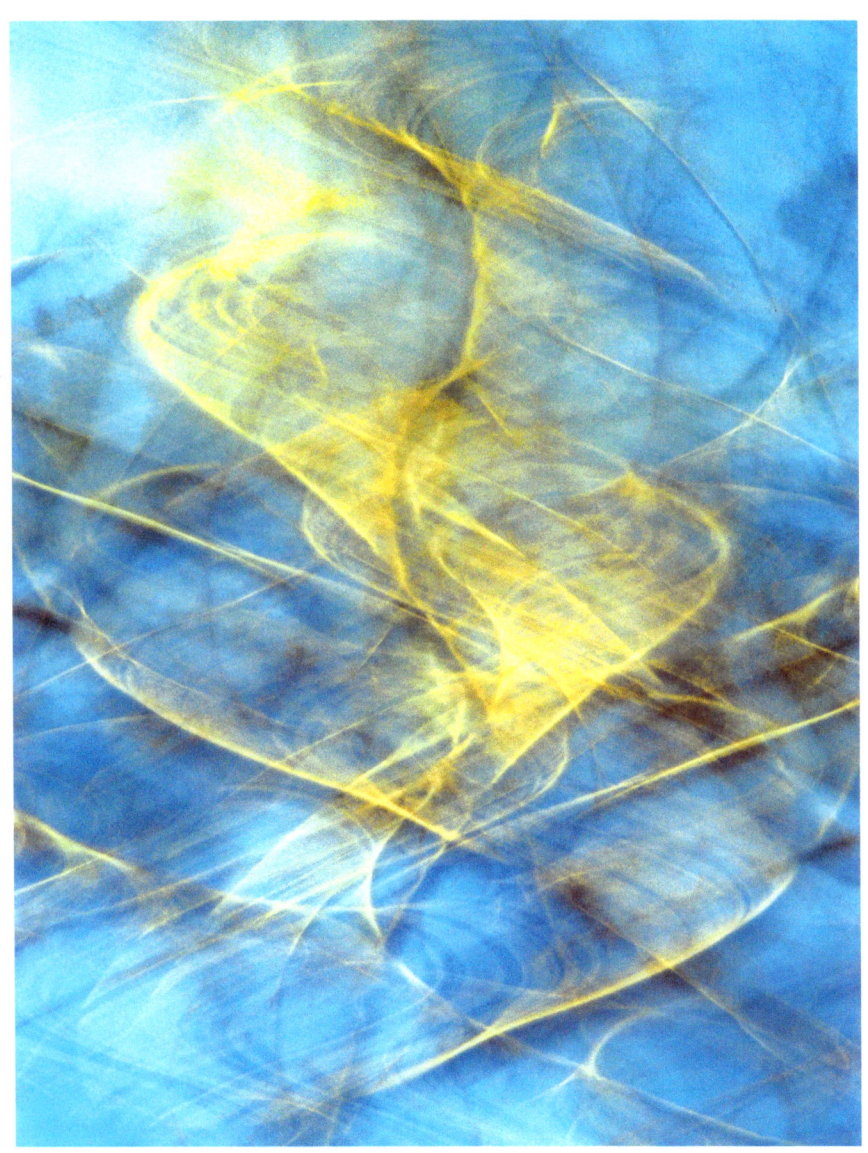

Maze DNA

Leaning back, he stared up to the violet sky, as if looking for an answer to his thoughts. Soto realized the darkening had not only been by chance, but also by choice, for thick clouds of movement had covered the array of magical sights in the watchful sky. The winds tightly sharpened as the sights and sounds of the heavens were magnified and illuminated by a settling storm. As restless winds whipped around him, they caught the golden tip of the flute protruding from his pocket and caused it to sing once again its mystical music. The wisps of music were caught by Nature's movement and swirled upwards as cumulus clouds from above spiraled downwards. Meeting in the middle, the two melded perfectly into a mighty force of Nature.

Soto's burlap sack was torn from his grasp, and he was swept off his feet into the night, as this storm, who knew not the fear of restriction, twisted through the lightning-lit landscape, transforming the traditional vistas of the countryside.

Lasting the longest moment of Soto's life, the storm and song finally receded into the calming skies high above the weather-worn surface below.

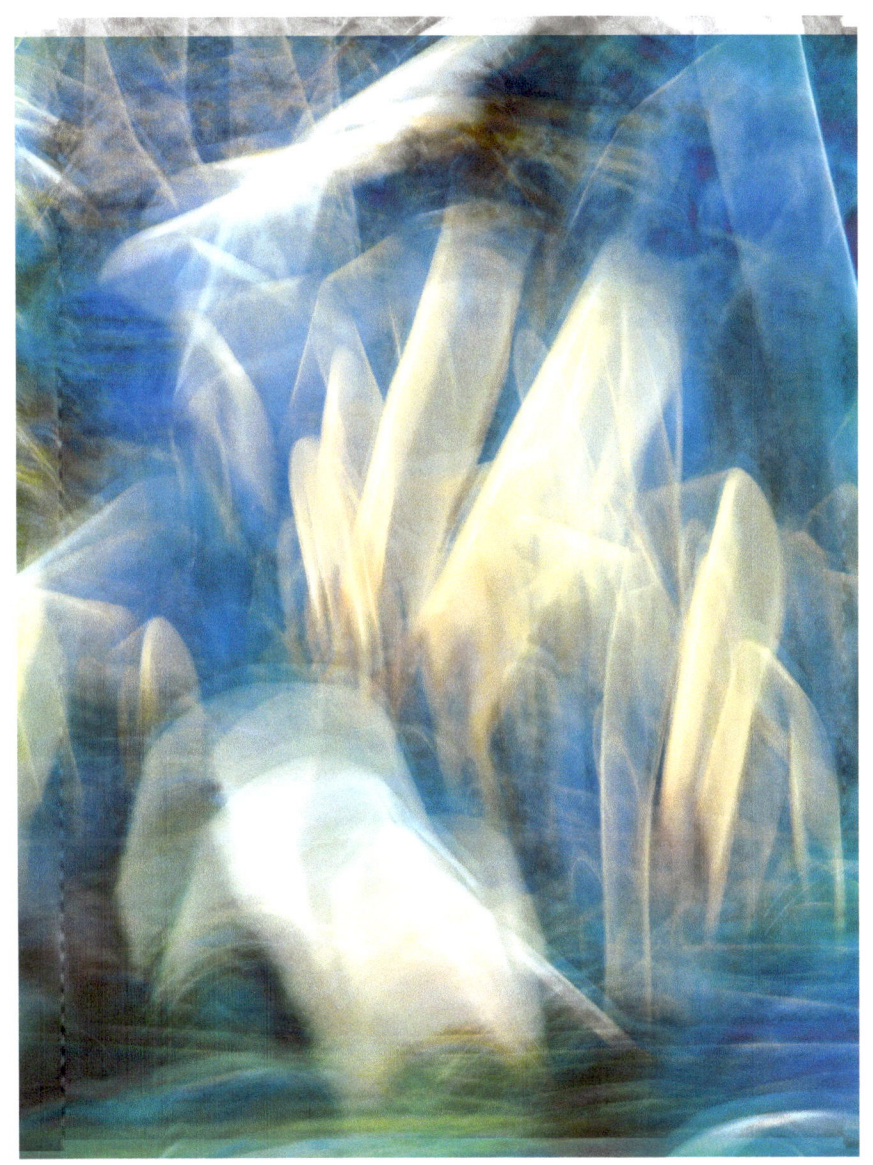

Crystal Cave

Waking from his dreams of enchantment, Soto blinked dew from his lashes and stared into the morning mural of painted skies. Colors danced in his eyes as a smile spread across his face. To Soto there was no better way to wake up than through the reality created by his unity with Mother Nature and her amazing instincts of happiness.

He stood where he had arisen and gazed over a countryside radically altered from the night before.

There was a sizable swath carved through the forest, clearing Soto's way to his destination.

His patched sack of treasures was nowhere to be seen, and the flute had vanished.

Breathing in a promise of adventure, he proceeded through the clearing towards the village, empty-handed, but with a head full of possibilities.

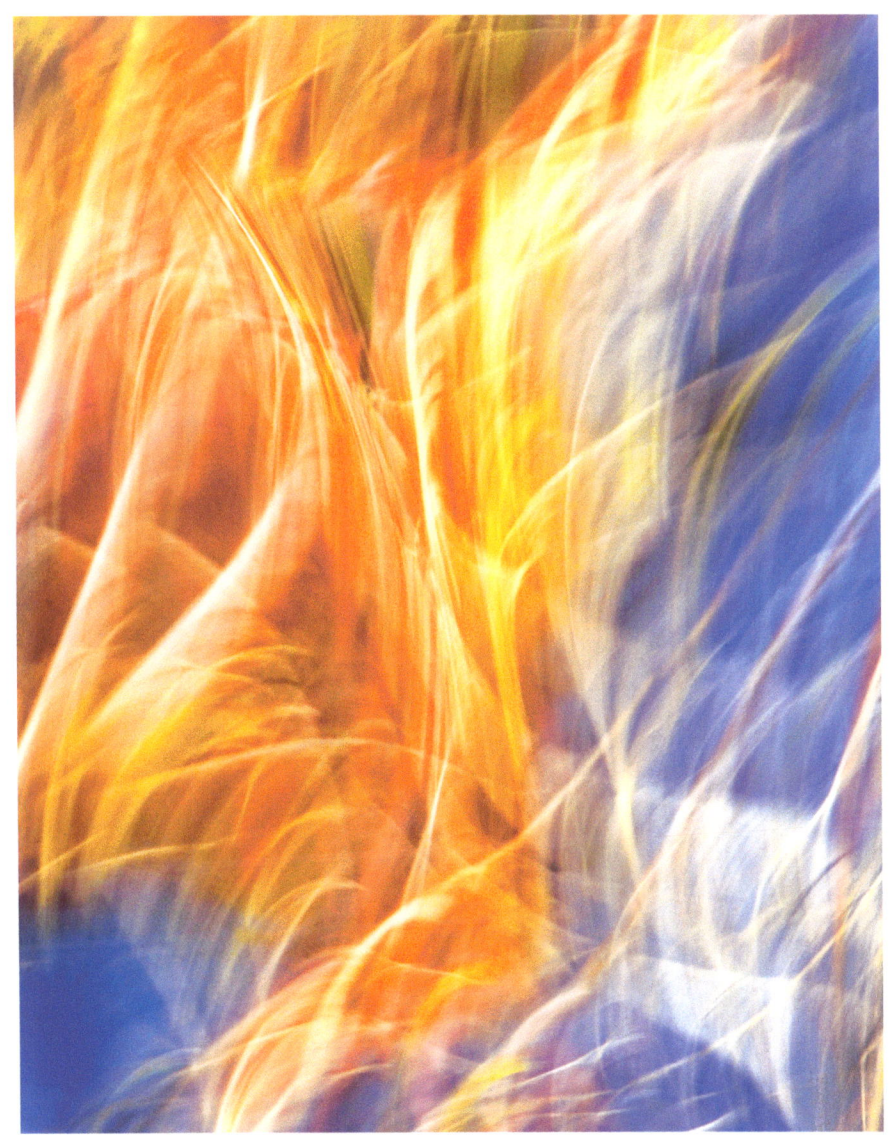

Transformation

The nomadic sun soon caught up with Soto and allowed his shadow to lead the way to the edge of the village, where pelicans perched on egg-laden nests on the peaked roofs of the quaint structures.

He could hear sounds of pleasant conversation between neighbors, cheerful laughter of children playing, sounds of animals who carried hope to their owners, a chorus of village life dancing through the cobblestone streets.

He could see the dyed colors of the shop windows displaying works of the craftsmen, smell freshly floured breads of the bakers, and feel twinges of curiosity speak to his imagination.

Soto stood and absorbed the scene around him.

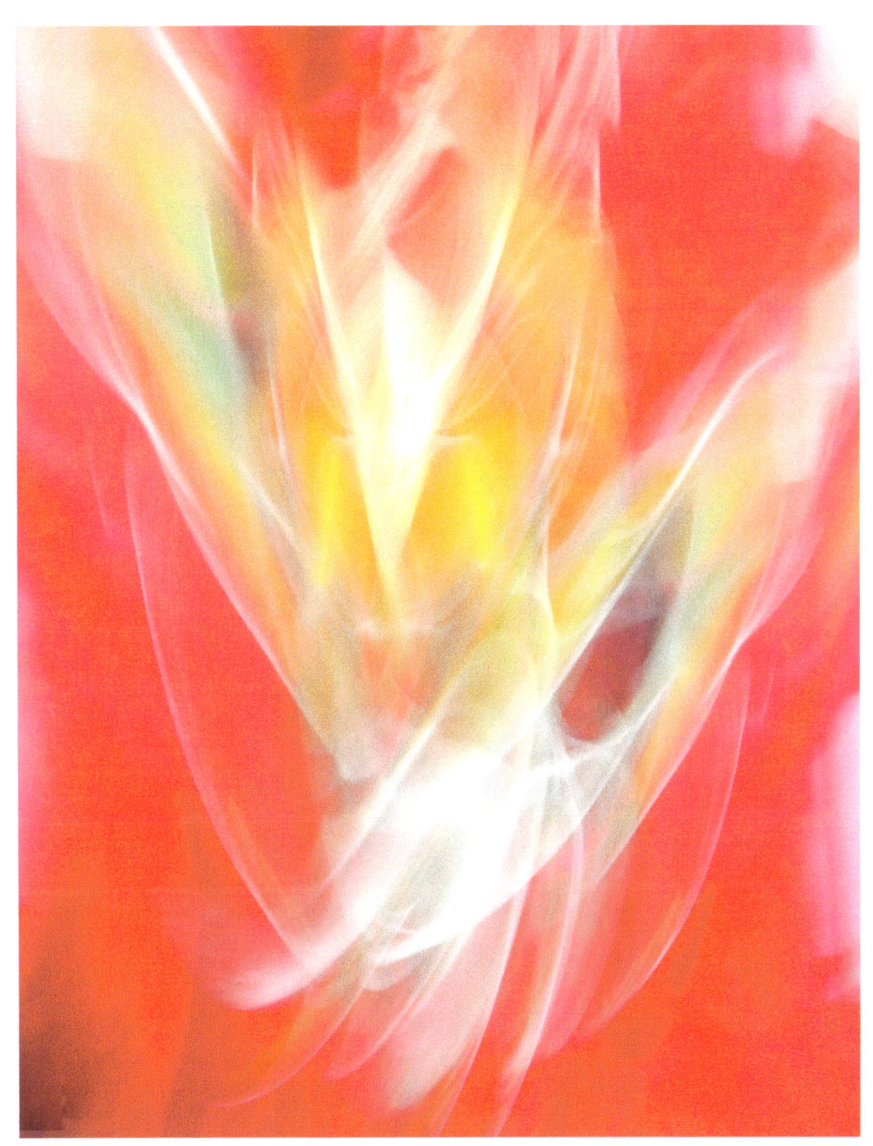

Lift Off

Wonder soon grabbed hold of the scattered children and pulled them to where Soto stood. Even in this village, where curiosities were common, this was something that called to their attention, and they pleaded for a story from the stranger.

Soto settled himself and began the story of his forest home, his discovery of the flute, of his magical journey to their village, the gifts that he was bringing to return to them, and how his flute and their treasures were lost. They were captivated by his tale of beauty, Nature, and magic.

As he finished his story, the entire village had gathered round to experience him. Scanning the crowd, he realized how it had affected their hearts, by their smiles, their tears, reflecting his own in the flames of the setting sun.

Most of the people had never been outside the borders of the village and therefore had not known the sensations Soto imparted. He stirred deep longings of adventure that had dwelt within them all.

One of the villagers stepped from the crowd and offered his home for the evening for the stranger to rest. Soto graciously accepted.

The townspeople dispersed. By this time it had grown quite dark, and the skies were illuminated once again by silent stars, but not as bright on this night, because low lanterns that lit the streets with their yellow-orange glow stole some of the darkness that had caused their brilliance to burn brighter.

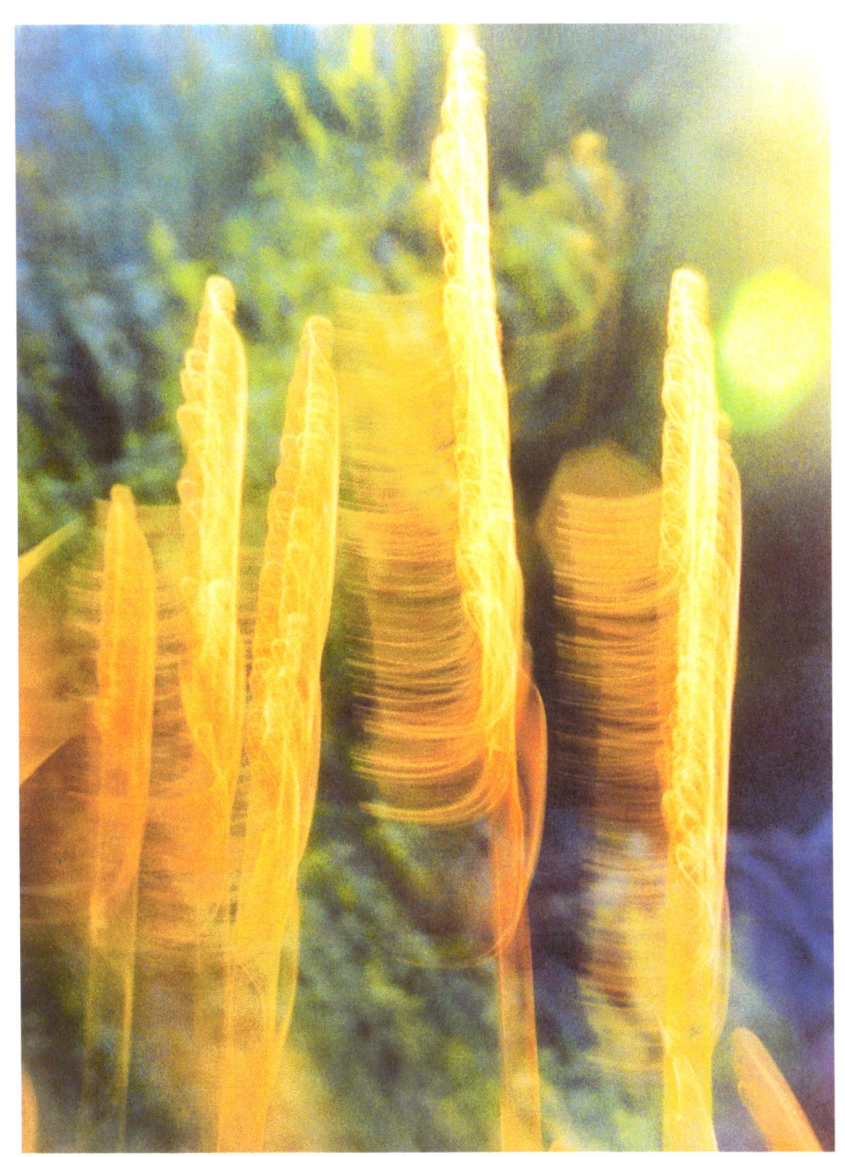

Spirit Dance

The morning sun broke the silence that had settled over a weary village. Darkness dried up in puddles of shade collecting in the recesses of shops, as light flooded the barren streets.

Soto awoke to the strangeness of surroundings that, although comforting, made him long for his forest home. This was the first morning in his life when he had not been awakened by the sounds of the forest, and a stirring in his heart pulled him up and out into the now-bustling streets.

He proceeded to the edge of the village, while townspeople gathered to bid farewell to their fleeting friend. Soto thanked them for their kindness, friendship and experience, but he knew his heart belonged where it resonated with the rhythms of the natural world.

A newfound freedom was realized as he waved and walked away from the sights and sounds of village life.

Whistling music from the sparrows, as he traveled down a different path to the same destination from which he had come, Soto felt harmonies within pulling him onwards to new heights of wonder in song.

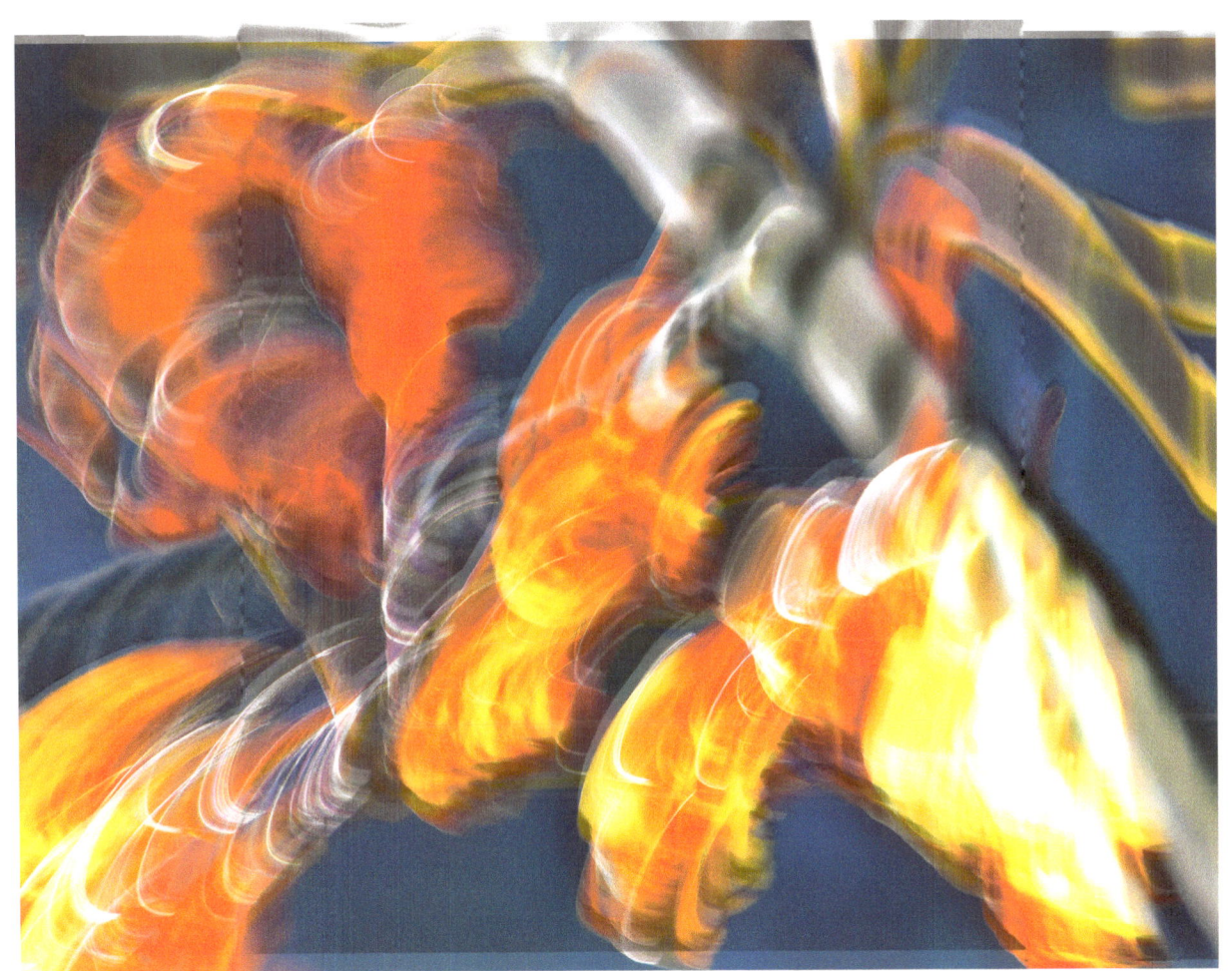

Reach

*I*n a brief distance, he could see sounds of movement, as a field of wildflowers erupted with a vibrant array of butterfly colors, as playful fawns pranced through the fragrance of fresh blossoms. Soto soon found himself enveloped by a menagerie of magnificence, for every color of the spectrum swam through the space around him. His heart took flight on the wings of the butterflies, with feelings found in this moment of amazement.

His mind, heart, and motion moved him to tears of joy at the happiness that had brought him to this place on his journey.

He loved how Nature made him feel whole in its presence.

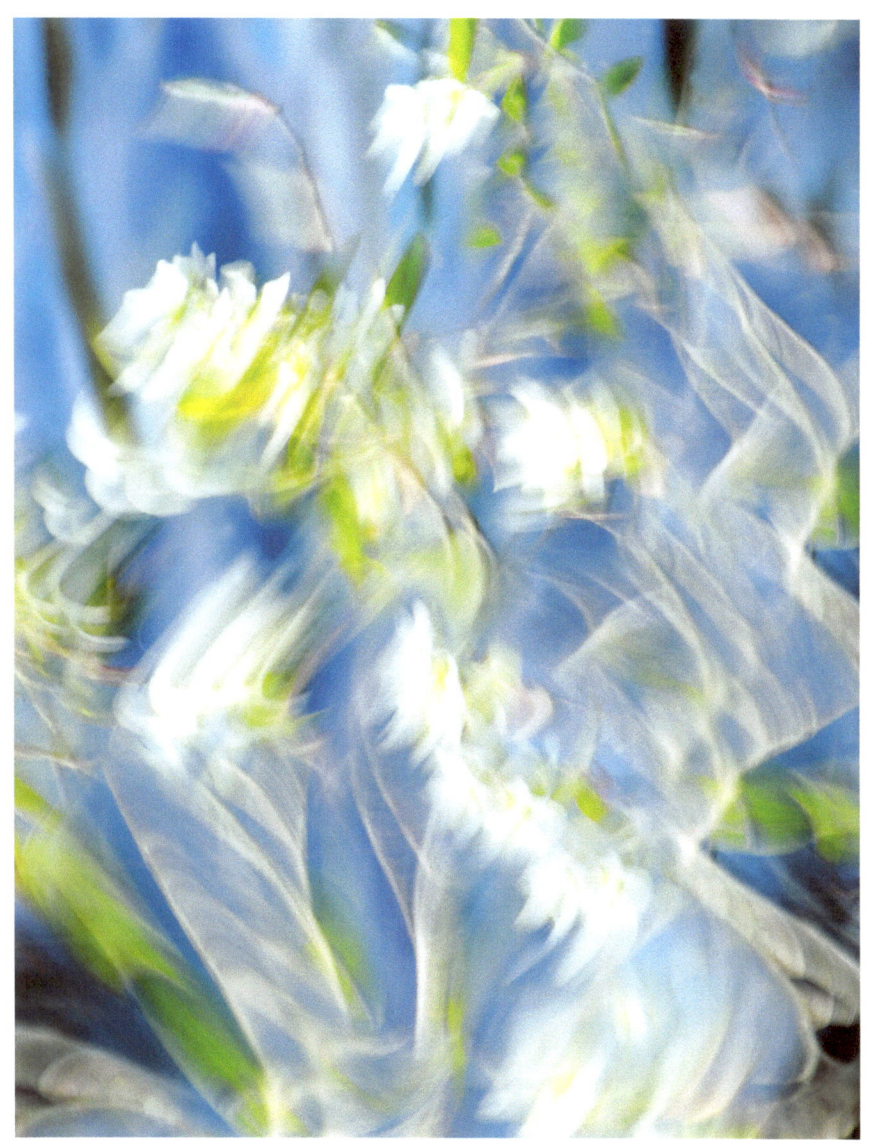

Spring

Soto moved merrily onwards through ever-changing country scenery and heard several new songs sung by the birds and bees that seemed to migrate with him on his journey home.

Time and tide moved forward with Soto, who soon found himself walking through a fragment of forest lit by the shadows that brought shade to its grateful inhabitants.

With this scene also came the familiar noises of unnatural ruffian shouts, mixed with the natural growls of a hungry bear.

Soto hurried through huddled trees to a place where the sights matched the sounds of the fear he could feel. Peering through the safety of moss-laden vines, he saw the ruffians cornered by the thinning bear, who had yet to satisfy her appetite.

The gravity of this situation pulled an apple from an overhead branch, and it came to rest at Soto's feet. Listening to Nature's advice, he began gathering fruit from various trees and a handful of honeycomb from the buzzing hives, quickly accumulating a banquet fit for the finest of beasts.

He grabbed a honey-drenched apple and tossed it into the clearing, where it rolled until it bumped against the bear's giant hunger.

Reaching down, she scooped up the sweet-smelling sticky fruit and held it up to her senses. Another piece of fruit strayed across the clearing and drew the temptation of the bear further and further from the huddled ruffians and closer and closer to where Soto hid.

30

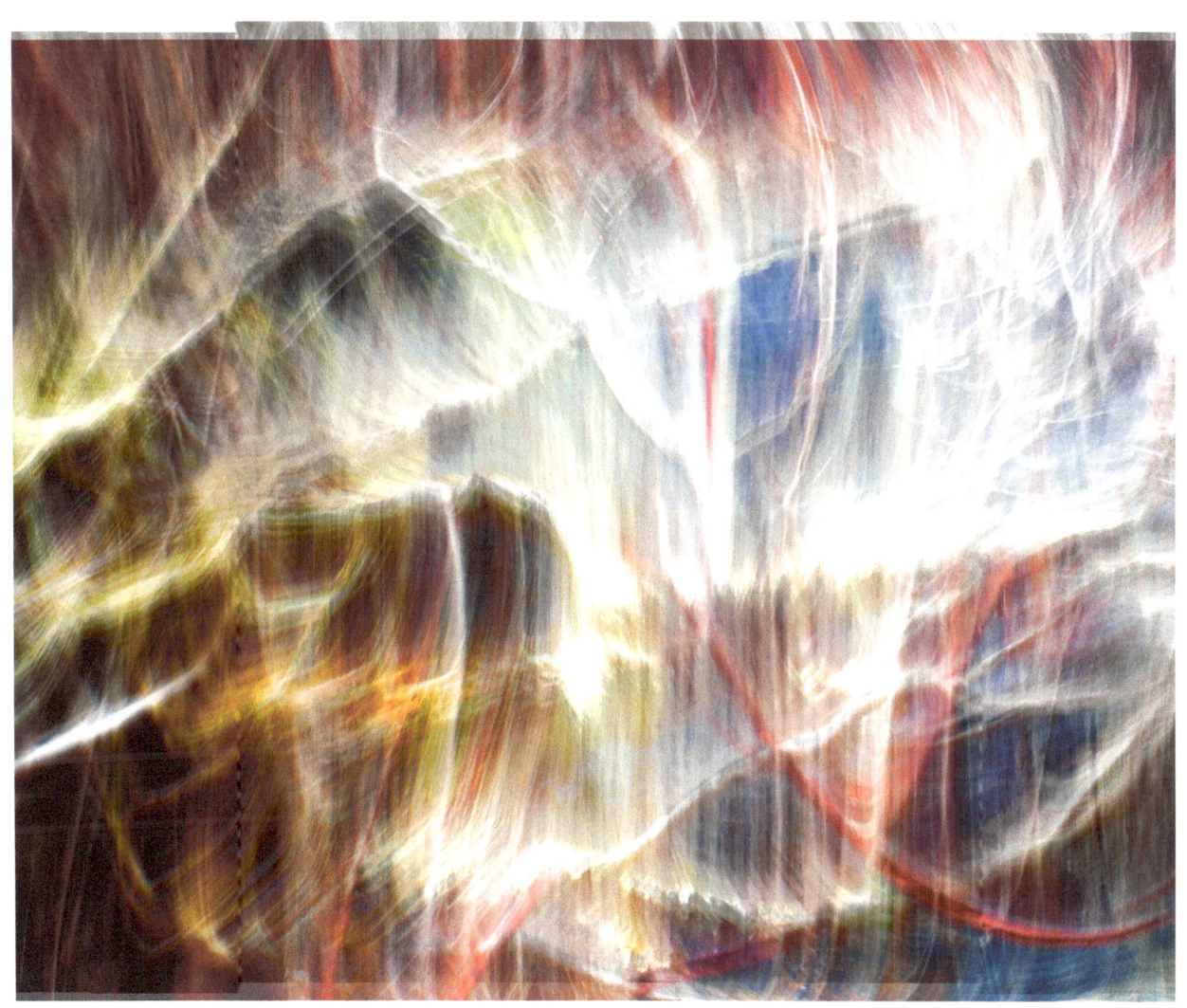

Here
Here

The grizzled bear devoured each piece of honey-drenched fruit as she followed her nose to the banquet prepared for her. Soto stood in shadows and watched the bear find her happiness in this simple gesture of kindness. He heard small sounds of padded feet exploring the scene. Into the clearing emerged two curious bear cubs, who knew only the comforts of their mother. They joined in the feast of fruit and honey until their famished thoughts were contented by a fullness of stomachs.

Soto watched as the bear family frolicked in dripping rays of a silver sun that trickled through the leaf-laden ceiling of their forest.

His happiness held him to that moment until the bears snuggled together and fell asleep from the fullness in their hearts.

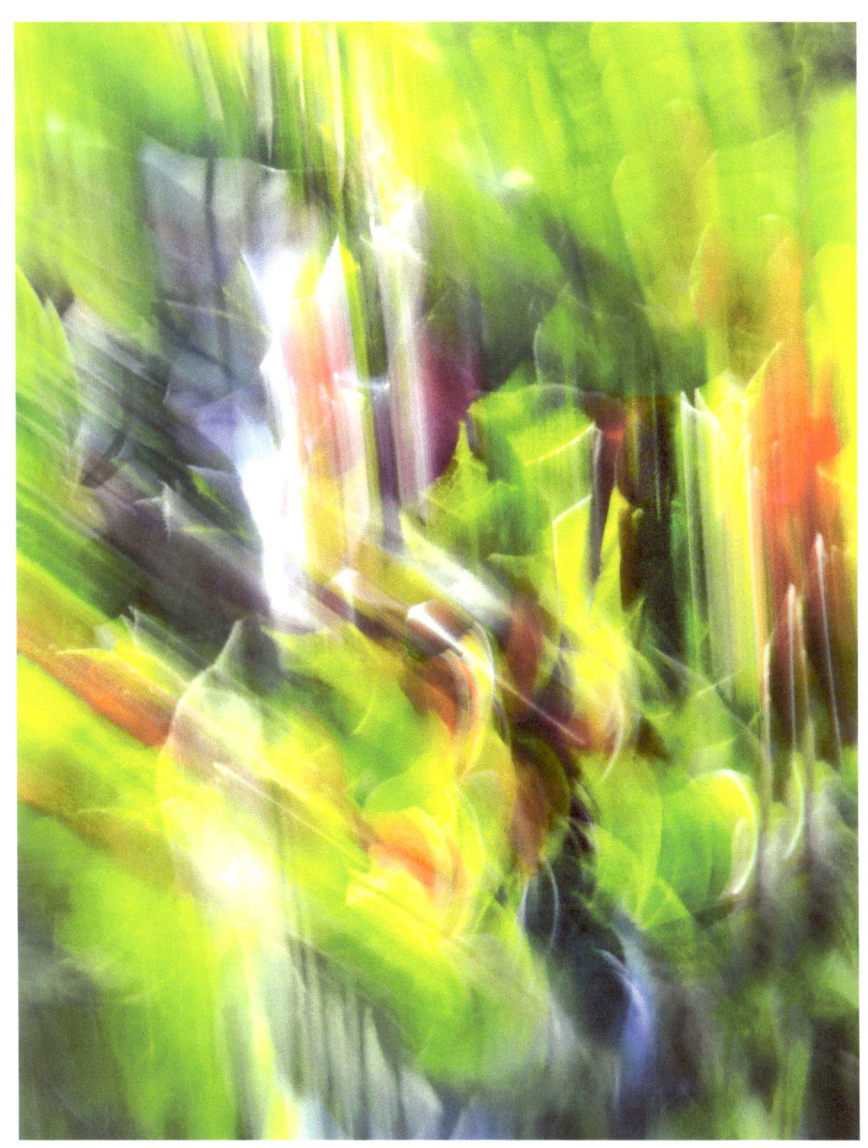

Holly

Soto turned to take his leave and found himself face to face with the ruffians, who were still pale-skinned from the fright of losing their freedom. The anger and ferocity had melted away, and their faces now held feelings of gratefulness for Soto's kindness. They extended their sun-scarred hands in an offering of peace, which Soto graciously accepted. An exchange was made of the only thing each had to offer—their thankfulness for each other.

Parting ways in the directions their desires were calling them, Soto smiled at their prospects.

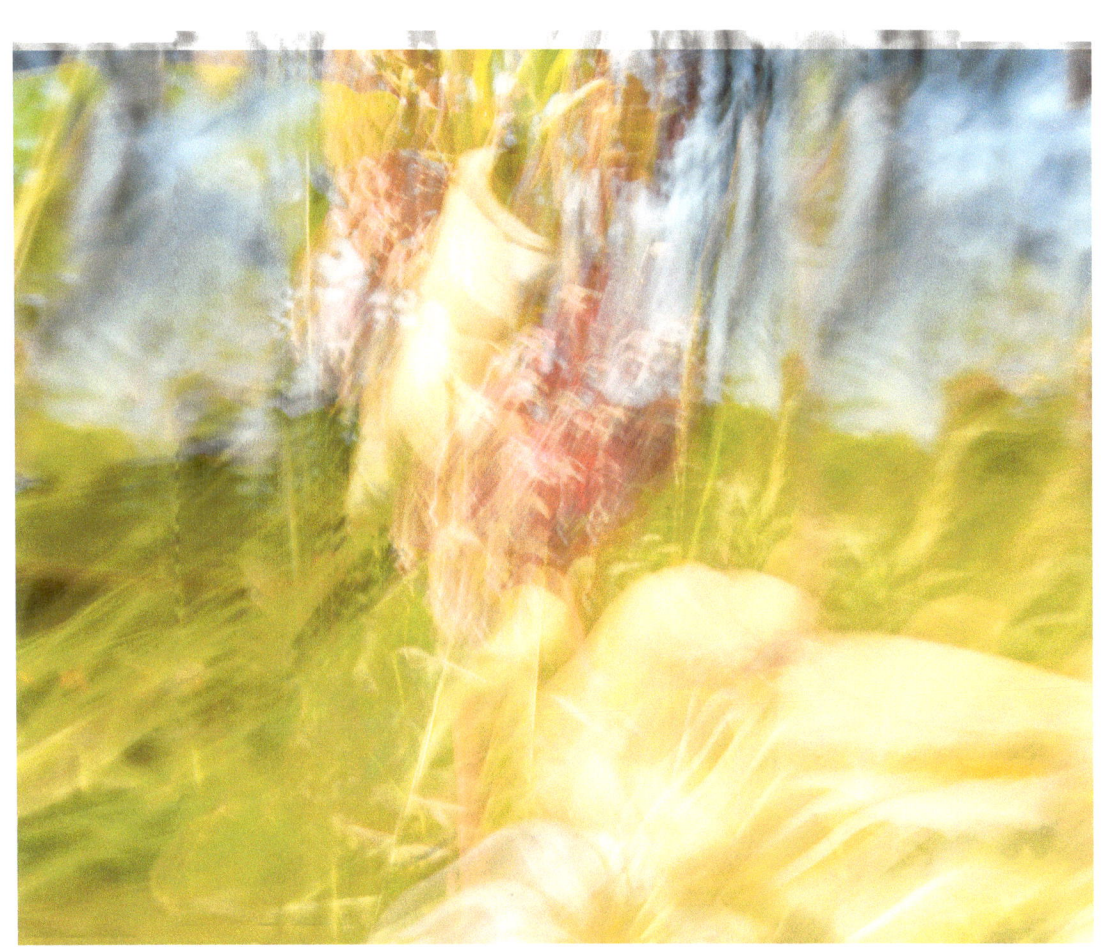

Summer Rush

Making his way up an untrodden path, his thoughtful musings and an intuitive dove guided him in the direction home.

Gathering his thoughts on this experience, Soto noticed Nature reflecting the scene once again, while clouds accumulated in darkening skies. He could see his forest in the near future and quickened pace as the silent clouds solidified over their velvet indigo canvas.

He could feel moisture in the air and his own senses heighten, and the sky above poured its beautiful, pure life into the open arms of Earth below.

Soto danced with delight, as more and more possibilities splashed down upon his smiling face. His heart did more than sing; it radiated the light that he had soaked in from the sun and lit the landscape in heavenly shades of silver and gold.

The Wind's and Nature's words carried him to the edge of his forest space, which knew not the boundaries of time.

Soto was dripping with life and openly embraced by his forest home. The forest life was covered with tears of joy for the return of the itinerant friend. Soto's tears streamed with Nature's as he made his way through grateful embraces from the flora and fauna of his sylvan friends.

Piercing through the clearing clouds and crystal droplets of rain, the sun reflected Soto's thoughts, illuminated the atmosphere with radiant colors of the purest ribbon of rainbow, stretching for miles into perfection, and cast a mystical glow over the lush hues of life that lit Soto's dreams from within.

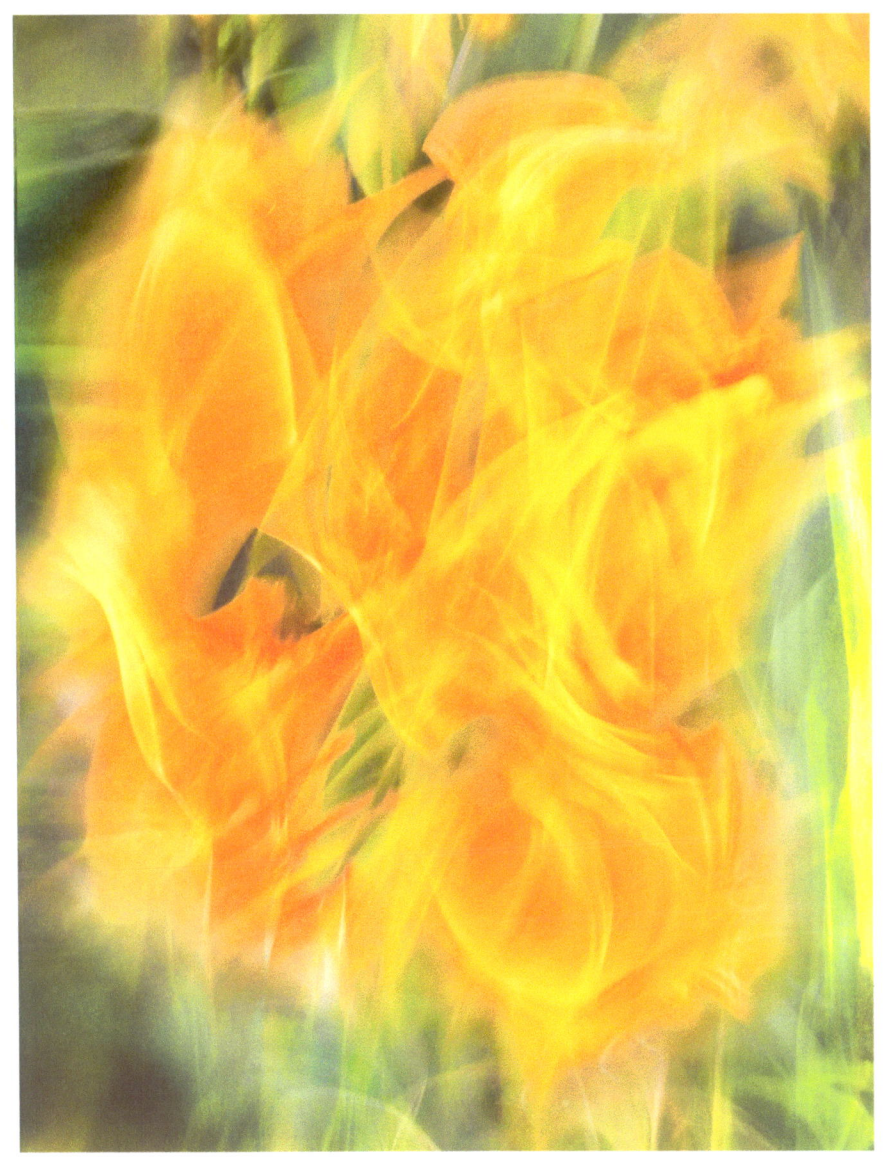

Lily Dance

Soto melded back into the blue-green mosses and tall grass of the forest floor, staring deeply into a setting sky, harmonizing with the birds and frogs, as they sang the sun to sleep, awakening the nightlife of fireflies, silver stars and iridescent moon, which illuminated the newly remembered reality of his dreams.

Opening his eyes to the sight of the peacock fluttering overhead, Soto Esphia knew the sensations of pure happiness.

The Beginning

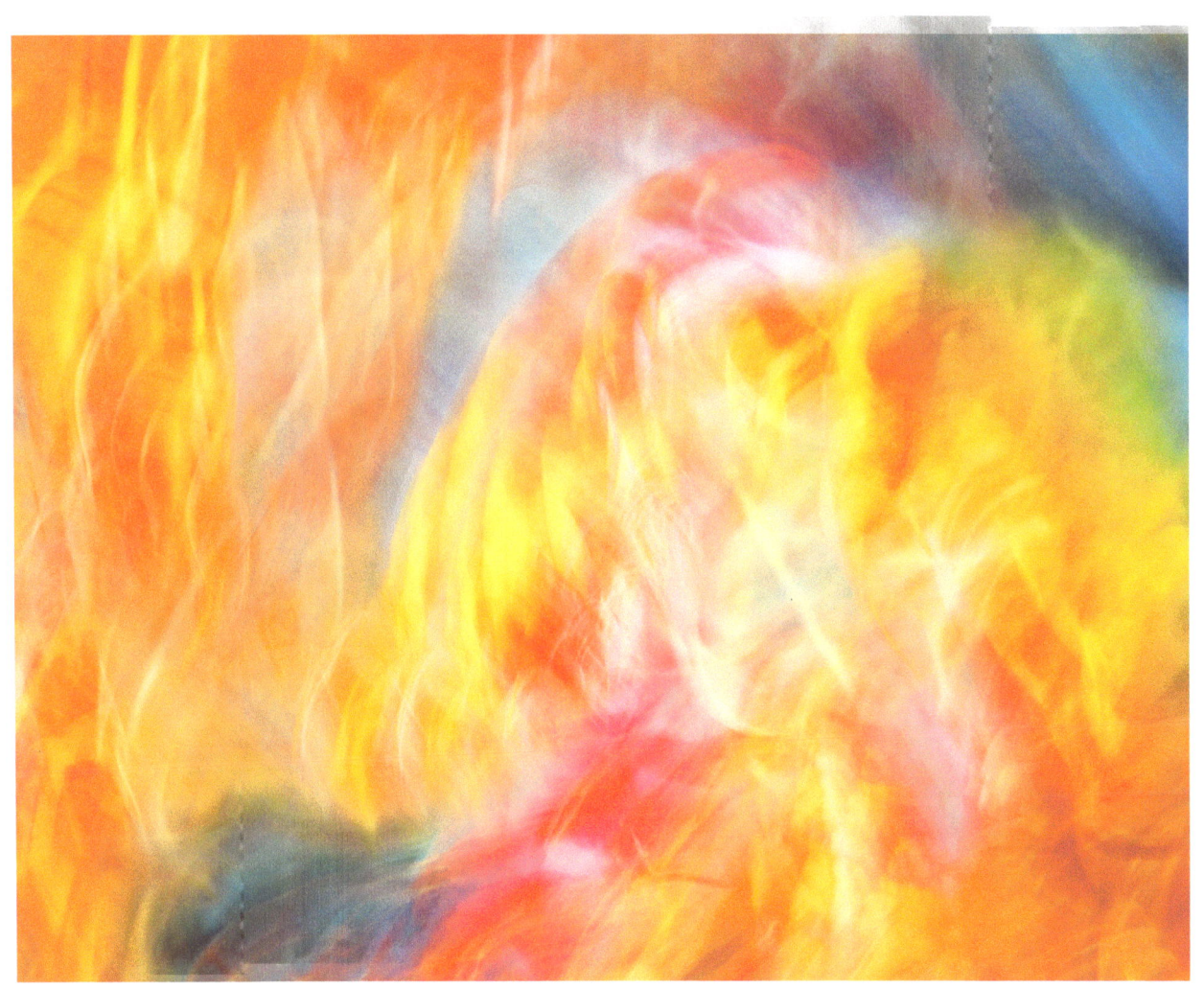

Fall

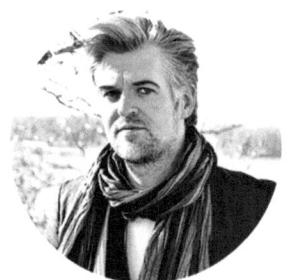

Dave Kroner researches esoteric and ancient traditions, reinterpreting the wisdom into his writings. View his full biography at polarbearandco.com/authors.

Ramona du Houx uses the camera with a painter's eye. Her technique involves movement to create a sense of wonder through colors, textures, memories, and the seasons. The images are dreamlike, healing, Zen meditative, and thought-provoking. All the photographic art was created on nature walks.

"Sometimes, when people look at my work, they relax and find tranquility, as by taking time to be at peace in Nature. At other times, the images can refresh, excite, or energize. I hope to connect viewers with Nature's magic by revealing her complex balance."

Ramona has been a photographer since her teens, She exhibits her work internationally. In Japan, she is represented by Gallery Storks of Tokyo. In Rockland, Maine, Gallery Fukurou shows her work.

photographybyramonaduhoux.com.

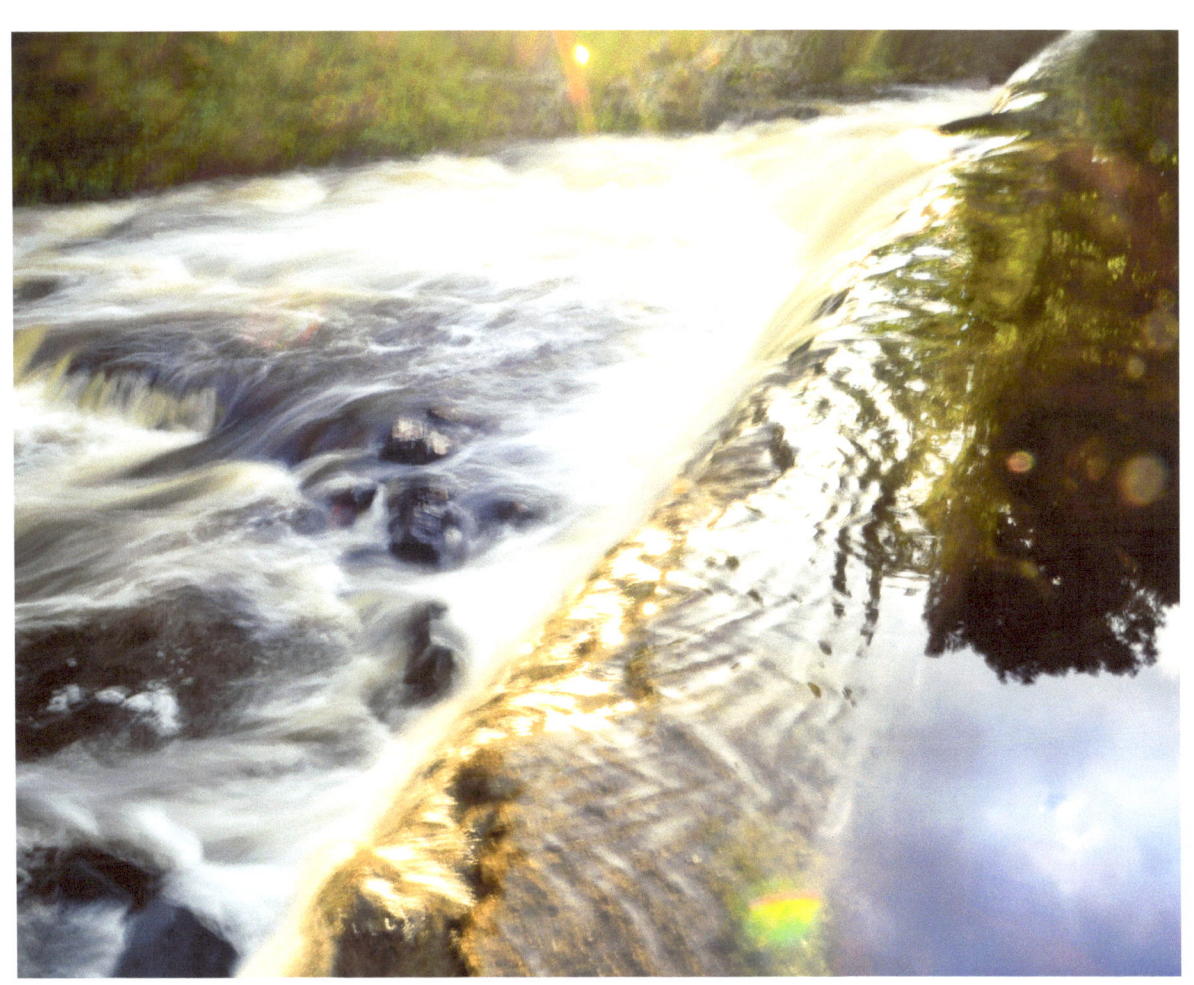

Waterfall Break

www.ingramcontent.com/pod-product-compliance
Lightning Source LLC
Chambersburg PA
CBHW051926210526
45473CB00006B/2148